Also from GHF Press

*Making the Choice: When Typical School
Doesn't Fit Your Atypical Child*

Forging Paths: Beyond Traditional Schooling

*If This is a Gift, Can I Send it Back?
Surviving in the Land of the Gifted and Twice Exceptional*

**Look for these Authors
Coming Soon from GHF Press
www.giftedhomeschoolers.org/ghf-press/**

Pamela Price of "Red, White & Grew"
Balancing Work & Real Life with Homeschooling

Corin Goodwin and Mika Gustavson
Gifted Homeschooling and Socialization

Jen Merrill of "Laughing at Chaos"
Challenges Facing Parents of Gifted and 2e Children

Learning in the 21st Century
How to Connect, Collaborate, and Create

By Ben Curran and Neil Wetherbee

Edited by Sarah J. Wilson

Published by GHF Press
A Division of Gifted Homeschoolers Forum
1257 Siskiyou Blvd. #174
Ashland, OR 97520

ISBN-13: 978-0615737881 (GHF Press)

ISBN-10: 0615737889

Cover design by Shawn Keehne (skeehne@mac.com).

Dedications

To Annabel, Bennett, and Leo
and
To Desiree, Ada, and Hazel

We hope we've taught you as much as you've taught us.

Contents

Acknowledgments

We have to start by thanking our wives, Corinne and Cassie. Without their help and support, none of our work would be possible. They are wonderful partners and mothers, and they never cease to amaze us.

We also want to thank the folks at Gifted Homeschoolers Forum, especially Corin Goodwin and Sarah Wilson, for giving us the opportunity to share our ideas about teaching and learning with homeschool families.

Finally, a special thanks goes out to our parents, David Morris and Pam Curran and Thomas and Deb Wetherbee. They were our first teachers and they continue to influence and encourage us to this day.

Authors' Note

What you're holding is more than just a book. It's a ticket to an interactive learning experience!

Be sure to follow our blog, our Facebook page, and our Twitter feed. Have a question? Stuck on something? Need extra support? Just reach out via one of those platforms or email us and we'll be in touch. Your success is important to us. We are here to help!

Blog: www.engagingeducators.com/blog

Twitter: www.twitter.com/engaginged

Facebook: www.facebook.com/engagingeducators

Email: contact@engagingeducators.com

Introduction

Imagine for a moment that you let all of the changes of the past 30 years pass you by. No Internet. No cell phones. No DVDs. No Facebook. No cable TV. No GPS. And so on. Can you imagine how different your life would be?

Now consider this: Our nation's education system has remained the same for not just the past 30 years, but perhaps the past 100! The world has transformed on an epic scale. Our schools have not. This could be one reason you have decided to homeschool your children. It's certainly one of the biggest motivators in our quest to help transform teaching and learning. (Our own six kids are our other biggest motivators!)

We've been working in education for a combined 20+ years and we believe learning should be fun. We believe it should be collaborative. We believe kids deserve to be connected with other kids from different regions and cultures. And, we believe they deserve the opportunity to be *creators*, instead of *consumers*, of academic content and information. We also believe that as a homeschooler, you have all the freedom that educators in traditional settings do not. Why not harness that power and discover the value of 21st century learning and the excitement of connected, collaborative, student-centered learning? Why not devote yourself to preparing your children to enter a world vastly different from the one you entered after high school and college? Your children, and ours, will be expected to know how to do things our schools aren't teaching. We are happy to serve as your guides.

Think of this book as your manual for building a 21st century learning experience. It is our goal to provide you and your children with enough ideas and inspiration to connect, collaborate, and create. Whether you're tech savvy or a novice, we want to not only teach you how to make these things happen, but to also push you to re-imagine the possibilities of learning in the 21st century.

Here's how we'll do it:

In the first section of this book, *Connect*, we share ideas for connecting with other homeschoolers and families via social media outlets such as blogs and Twitter.

Once you're connected with other families, we show you in *Collaborate* how to engage in collaborative educational experiences with people across town or across the globe.

Finally, in *Create*, we provide descriptions of several online tools your children can use to create digital learning artifacts (explained later), as well as detailed explanations of some digital projects we've tried with students to help you get started.

As you read, we encourage you to have your computer nearby, so that you can try out the ideas we're going to share with you. Also, be sure to use the space at the end of each section for note-taking. Feel free to dive right in to everything discussed, or try one new idea at a time and become really comfortable with it before adding a second idea to your 21st century homeschool experience. With this text as your handbook, you'll be ready to transform your home learning environment and transport you and your children on an exciting journey that will hopefully last a lifetime.

Connect

The 21st century offers many learning opportunities to homeschooling families. Chief amongst these is the opportunity to connect with other families from around the world. There are several easy—and free—ways to do this. Why is connecting so important for homeschooling families? The answer is simple: when we learn together, our learning and our teaching improve.

Your current personal learning network (PLN) probably consists of homeschooling friends in your community or region. When you get together, you trade stories and ideas, learning from each other. Talking about teaching and learning can be great fun. If you're like us, it's one of your favorite things to do.

You probably also read homeschool publications and articles. Maybe every once in awhile, you read a blog post. These are great ways to learn, too. They count as part of your learning network, just like the people you talk to do.

Still, while your current PLN is surely valuable, if you aren't taking advantage of current means of connecting with homeschoolers from around the world, you are missing out on a vast amount of information and inspiration. With just a small amount of effort, you can expand your PLN by a factor of 100 or more. The learning that is taking place in your home will subsequently improve by an equal, or even greater, margin. Once you are a connected homeschooling family, you will be amazed by how much more confident and passionate *you* feel, and how much more excited and engaged *your children* feel.

In this section, we'll discuss four easy ways to connect with and learn from others: Subscribing to blogs with Google Reader, using Twitter, social bookmarking with Diigo, and creating your own blog with Blogger.

Subscribing to Blogs with Google Reader

Reading blogs can be a great source of information, inspiration, and ideas. There are thousands of homeschoolers sharing via blogs. While there are too many to follow them all, with the help of Google Reader, you can subscribe to just the ones you like best, and have all the content delivered directly to you. No more searching. No more scrolling through page after page looking for useful content. All of the resources that you like best get delivered straight to your easy-to-navigate Google Reader page.

Here's a quick list of blog articles we encountered while spending just a few moments scrolling through our blog subscriptions:

- Should you join a homeschool co-op?

- Using the right tone when constructively criticizing your kids

- Helping children maintain deeper, sustained investigations

- A great example of a project involving the book *Alphabet City,* by Stephen T. Johnson

- A description of a science mini-unit on blood

- A mom sharing photos of her family "classroom"

- Tips for planning homeschool lessons

Once you find a collection of great blogs to subscribe to, you will never be disappointed. Rare is the day when, after spending just 10 minutes checking our blog subscriptions, we don't find at least one thing of value. We recommend making blog reading a habit, perhaps while you sip your coffee in the morning or during your lunch break. Find a regular time in your daily schedule to work it in. If you commit to making it a part of your routine, you'll quickly become hooked. A commitment to regular reading is an important first step, because without it, the time you invest in setting up your Google Reader will be for naught.

Another great thing about blogs is that they are also interactive publications. They offer the opportunity for readers to comment and ask questions. Leaving a comment on a blogger's post is a great way to engage the blogger in an expanded conversation. This enables connections to happen between blogger and reader, and as these conversations grow, your PLN will expand.

Here is how to make connections with bloggers worldwide by subscribing to blogs with Google Reader.

Finding and Subscribing to Blog Feeds

RSS, short for "Really Simple Syndication" or "Rich Site Summary" depending on whom you ask, provides instant updates of websites that change frequently, such as blogs, news headlines, podcasts, etc. These updates, thanks to RSS "feeds," are delivered directly to subscribers via a tool called a feed reader. Subscribing to RSS feeds through a feed reader can bring countless resources to your attention, allowing you to stay up-to-date with homeschooling trends. Feeds also serve as an excellent source of ideas and inspiration. Our feed reader of choice is Google Reader. You can access Google Reader at www.google.com/reader.

First, you will need to be able to locate and subscribe to feeds. We'll focus mainly on homeschooling blogs, but these steps can be used for any site with a feed.

Locating Feeds (a.k.a. Finding Stuff to Read)

You can find feeds to subscribe to in one of three ways:

1. Use Google Reader's search option

2. Directly paste in the URL

3. Subscribe directly from the webpage

Use Google Reader's search option

Google Reader offers two ways to search for feeds: a search field on the "Subscribe" page and the "Browse for stuff" tool.

To use the search field, log in to www.google.com/reader. (Note that you will need a free Google account before you can log in.) On the page that opens after logging in, click the "Subscribe" button to open a search field. You simply enter search terms such as "writing" or "NPR" or "educational technology" or "homeschool" or "gifted." This search will provide you with a list of matching blogs, to which you'll be able to subscribe with one click. Once you click the "subscribe" button, you will automatically receive updates each time the blogger posts new content. The blog's name will then appear in the "Subscriptions" menu in the sidebar (the list of options that always appears on the side of any Google Reader page).

Google Reader's "Browse for stuff" tool can be accessed from the sidebar. Clicking this link will give you the option to search or to receive some subscription recommendations. Just make sure you've subscribed to at least one blog first. The recommendations are based upon your current subscriptions. So if you don't have subscriptions, you won't get recommendations. You can also find recommendations in the "Explore" section of the sidebar.

Directly paste in the URL

Know a blog to which you want to subscribe? Just click that "Subscribe" button, paste its URL (web address, such as http://engagingeducators.com/blog) into the field, and click the enter key. You'll automatically be subscribed and the feed will be added to your subscriptions menu.

Subscribe directly from the webpage

Sometimes, if a webpage has an RSS feed, you can subscribe directly from the page. How do you know if a page has an RSS feed? You can look for the letters "RSS" or the words "feed" or "subscribe." Also keep an eye out for the universal RSS icon (an orange square with the white radio waves): . Any page that has this icon on it has an RSS feed.

You can also be on the lookout for a button that says "Add to Google" or something similar. Clicking this button will lead you through a short series of steps to add the site's feed to your Google Reader page.

Finding Great Feeds

Look for Blogrolls. Many bloggers keep a list of their favorite blogs in their sidebar. This list, called a blogroll, is a great way to find new blogs. If you like the blog you're reading, you might like some of the blogs the blogger links to.

Great Blogs to Follow for Learning as a Family

Gifted Homeschoolers Forum Blogroll
    http://giftedhomeschoolers.org/blogs/

Wonderopolis
    http://wonderopolis.org

The Kid Should See This
    http://thekidshouldseethis.com

The New York Times Learn Network
    http://learning.blogs.nytimes.com/

CNN Student News
   http://cnnstudentnews.blogs.cnn.com/

PBS News Hour Extra
   http://www.pbs.org/newshour/extra/

All the blogs at How Stuff Works
   http://blogs.howstuffworks.com/

Scientific American podcasts (Listen to audio or read the transcripts)
   http://www.scientificamerican.com/podcast/

Google Reader Essentials

By now you're subscribing to several blogs and feeds using Google Reader. Eventually, your RSS feeds might prove overwhelming and difficult to navigate. Google Reader offers several features to reduce these problems. Here are four things you should know about and use:

1. The home page

2. Your subscriptions

3. Managing subscriptions

4. Subscribing as you surf

The home page

This is what you see when you see whenever you open Google Reader. It shows you which of your subscriptions have the newest items and gives previews of these items. Click on the feed's name to open it and show all its recent posts, or click directly on the post. To return to this view at any time, click the "Home" link in the sidebar.

Your subscriptions

All the sites you subscribe to are listed in the sidebar. The number of unread items is noted in parentheses. Clicking on any one of the feed names will take you to a list of the feed's items, with the unread items highlighted in bold. Clicking on an individual item will open it (and clicking it again will close it). Some blog feeds display the full article in Google Reader, others give you a portion of it, requiring you to click on the item's blue title to go to the actual blog and read the rest. Clicking the little gray box with the arrow in it will take you to the blog, too.

The menu bar that appears at the bottom of an open item offers some useful options:

- Clicking the star turns it yellow and marks this as a favorite item. This is useful for posts you want to remember or come back to later. This can also be done by clicking the star in front of the post's title. To see all items you've starred, click "Starred Items" in the sidebar.

- "+1" is Google's rendition of the "like" option you find on Facebook. If you give a post +1, it will show up on your Google+ profile (if you're a Google+ user). "Share" shares this site with people following you in Google Reader.

- "Email" allows you to email the post.

- "Keep Unread" does just that, keeping this post unread so that it stays visible within this subscription.

- "Add Tags" assigns categories to a post (similar to tags in Flickr or Diigo). You can then search or sort posts by tag.

Managing subscriptions

Your feed reader can get a little cluttered as your subscriptions start adding up. Google Reader allows you to stay organized by creating folders for your subscriptions. Start by hovering your mouse over the Subscriptions section of the sidebar. A little black triangle will appear to the right of the word "Subscriptions." Click it and choose "Manage Subscriptions." This will allow you to create "folders" to put your blog subscriptions into. For example, all your math feeds could go into a folder you create called "Math," and all your science feeds into a "Science" folder, and so on.

Once you've created folders, you can add new subscriptions to a folder in one of three ways: using "Manage subscriptions," dragging the new subscription into a folder in the subscriptions menu, or by clicking "Feed settings" when viewing an individual subscription and choosing the folder from the drop-down menu.

Subscribing as you surf

Google Reader offers a helpful bookmark button for your toolbar. Clicking it while you're looking at a site with a feed will add the subscription to Google Reader. To get this bookmark, click the gear in the upper right hand corner and choose "Reader settings." Next, click the "Goodies" tab. Then scroll down to "Subscribe as You Surf." Follow the directions to drag the "Subscribe..." link to your bookmarks toolbar.

RSS Tips and Tricks

1. At times, clicking on the RSS icon or on a link that says "Subscribe" or "Feed" will often bring up a page that looks like a jumbled mess of indecipherable code. If this is the case, you need to hit your browser's back button and follow these steps:

   a. Right click (ctrl+click for Apple) on the icon or feed link and select "Copy link address."

   b. Open Google Reader and click "Subscribe."

   c. Paste the link address into the field that appears and click the enter key. The feed will be added to your subscriptions.

2. Having trouble finding the RSS link? For some reason, some blogs and sites hide it at the very bottom of their home pages.

3. We definitely want to stress the importance of making your blog-reading an interactive experience. Do your best to make blogging a two-way street by leaving comments on the blog posts that you read. Whether it's a question, a statement of praise, or a criticism (politely stated, of course), blogs empower you to have a discussion with the author. It's a unique opportunity to connect, but a lot of people hesitate to do it.

4. Want a list of blogs to follow? Check out our bundle of homeschooling blogs which you can subscribe to with one click: http://bit.ly/homeschoolblogs.

IDEAS & INSPIRATION

Use this space to jot down your thoughts and ideas about subscribing to blogs.

_____

_____

_____

_____

_____

Using Twitter

Twitter is a micro-blogging platform used by millions worldwide. They give you 140 characters to answer the question: *What's happening?* Twitter is often regarded as little more than a time-waster or an outlet for tracking celebrities; however, it's about much more than finding out what your favorite pop star had for breakfast—it can change the way you help your children learn.

Why do you need Twitter? Twitter is yet another great way to connect with homeschoolers worldwide. It makes sharing resources quick and easy. Building a good group of tweeters to follow is a great way to improve your own learning and your teaching. Twitter has quickly become a unique and important way for homeschooling parents to connect, collaborate, and learn. Parents follow each other's posts, ask each other questions, share ideas, post links, and more.

Let us try to demonstrate the power of Twitter for you. Open the webpage www.twitter.com. In the search field, type #homeschool. This pound sign is a hashtag (more on these in a moment) and your search will reveal all of the recent tweets that were tagged "#homeschool."

When we tried this, here are some resources we discovered:

- How to use LEGOS™ in homeschooling

- A list of art and music resources

- "The ultimate guide to choosing homeschool curriculum"

- A new homeschool mother's reflection blog

- "The ultimate guide to creative writing resources"

And that is just the tip of the iceberg. With Twitter, resources just like that are delivered directly to you.

How is this different from Google Reader? We admit that they might sound similar in premise, but whereas Google Reader and blogs are great for the consumption of knowledge, they can be a bit of a one-way street when it comes to interaction. While you are able to leave comments, blogs are mainly designed to be *read*. Tweets are designed to be clicked, replied to, and shared. Twitter is a more immediately interactive tool for communicating with a network of homeschoolers.

In fact, think of Twitter as a conversation tool, sort of like a telephone. It's a way of talking to other homeschooling families about something that matters a great deal to you, the education of your children. In the case of Twitter, however, you don't pick up a phone and call one person, you send a 140-character message to thousands. Just imagine how powerful this could be if you were looking for math tips, field trip ideas, resource recommendations, or more. There's a vast amount of learning that can happen via Twitter. It's time you took the leap!

To get started, you'll need a Twitter account. Go to www.twitter.com and click "Sign Up Now." All you need to provide is your name and email address. You'll then choose a username and a password. You'll also be able to upload an image to serve as your profile picture and create a short bio of yourself, both which can be changed at any time.

There! That only took a couple of minutes. Now, you're ready to start tweeting!

Twitter Essentials

Your home page

You see your home page after logging into Twitter. From here you can read the posts (a.k.a. "tweets") of the people you follow, post a tweet of your own in the status update box, check to see who is following you, search, and more.

Your profile

Your profile looks a lot like your home page, except it shows only tweets you've sent. It's what people see when they click on your username. It has a unique URL: www.twitter.com/yourusername. (For example, our home page is www.twitter.com/engaginged and GHF's is www.twitter.com/GiftedHF.) Also, it shows some thumbnails of the people you follow. You can view the people following you and being followed by you, just by clicking on the numbers.

Following others

On your home page you see only the tweets of people you follow. Only the people that follow you see your tweets on their home page. The best way to get people to follow you is to follow them. If you find a user you'd like to follow, go to their profile and click "Follow." Their tweets will now appear on your home page.

Notes on following

- Having trouble discovering people to follow? Go to the profile of a tweeter you respect or enjoy. Click on the number of people they are following. This will show you a list of all the people they follow. Choose people you would like to follow from the list. You can do the same thing with the new people that you are now following.

- Not happy with someone you're following? You can always un-follow by clicking on the list of people you're following on your home page or profile, and then choosing "unfollow" from the drop down menu beside their name. This can also be done by going to their profile and doing the same thing.

@replies and mentions

An @reply is Twitter-speak for a reply to someone's tweet. If you want to reply to what someone tweets, hover your mouse over their tweet. It will turn blue. Simply click "Reply." This will automatically generate a pop-up window with their tweet but with the @ symbol and the person's username at the front.

A mention is a tweet that contains another user's username anywhere in the tweet. For example, you might tweet, "Really appreciate the help and support of @GiftedHF."

Notes on @replies and mentions

- @replies and mentions are *public*. They will appear on your profile page, in the feed of the person you mentioned, *and* the feed of anyone *who follows both you and that user.*

- @replies have the words "in reply to" at the bottom. If you click on the @reply, it will display the tweet the user @replied to.

- Twitter allows you to view all the tweets that mention you by username. Just click "@connect" at the top of the page and you'll see a list of all your "interactions." This includes every tweet that includes your username in any way, as well as tweets of yours that were retweeted or marked as a "favorite."

- If someone that you aren't following @replies to one of your tweets, it won't show up in your Twitter feed, but it will show up on your Connect page.

Favorites

Often, members of your Twitter network will share links to useful sites. Or, you might see a tweet that you like or want to remember. Twitter offers you the option of "marking" favorite tweets. To do so, hover over the tweet and click either the star or the word "Favorite."

To view your Favorites, click the "Favorites" link in the sidebar of your profile or home page.

Direct Messages

A Direct Message, or DM, is just that, a message sent directly to another Twitter user. This user *must be someone that is following you.* You can send DMs directly from the person's Twitter profile. Just click the drop down menu to the right of the Follow button.

Retweeting

If you see "RT" at the beginning of a tweet, this means it's a *retweet.* Simply put, a retweet is a tweet that is tweeted again by another user. Users retweet tweets that they find useful, valuable, or interesting so that everyone they follow can see it, too. A retweet amplifies the original tweet's impact by increasing the number of people who can access the original tweet. If you see a tweet you like or one that has a useful link, retweet it to share it with your Twitter network. There are two ways to do this:

1. Hover over the tweet and click "Retweet."

2. Copy and paste the tweet into your status update box. Be sure to put "RT" and the person's username (e.g., @engaginged or @GiftedHF) at the beginning of the retweet.

URL shortening

One of the most useful things to do within your Twitter network is to share links; however, some URLs are so long that they use up most or all of your 140 characters. Don't worry! When you use Twitter, all URLs will be automatically shortened to 20 characters. Several websites offer you the ability to shorten URLs even further and track the number of clicks they receive. Three popular URL shorteners are http://tinyurl.com, http://goo.gl, and http://bit.ly. Simply paste in the original URL, then copy and paste the shortened version into your tweet.

Hashtags

A hashtag is used to mark keywords or categories in a tweet. For example, if you post a homeschool-related tweet, you could add the hashtag "#homeschool." To add a hashtag to your tweet, be sure you precede it with the # symbol. Hashtags make it easier for other users to find your tweets via search. If you want to find recent tweets labeled with the #homeschool hashtag, type it into the search field of any Twitter page.

Notes on hashtags:

• Hashtags can appear anywhere in a tweet.

• Clicking on the hashtag in someone's tweet will show you all the recent tweets that have been tagged in the same way.

- The most popular homeschool-related hashtags are #homeschool, #hschat, and #hsbloggers. The most popular gifted-related hashtag is #gtchat.

HootSuite and TweetDeck

If you really get into Twitter, you might want to consider www.hootsuite.com or www.tweetdeck.com. These third-party applications each automatically update, and have easy-to-use interfaces and built-in URL shortening. In addition, each allows you to tweet from multiple Twitter accounts.

Check out http://bit.ly/hootsuitebasics for our guide to using Hootsuite.

Twitter accounts to follow

Now that you're using Twitter, you may want to start following some of the various gifted-, homeschool-, and education-related Twitter accounts. The Appendix contains a list of Twitter accounts for you to check out. Keep in mind, like anything on the Internet, these could change at any time. We recommend that you find a few you like, then follow some of the accounts they're following (see page 12 for more information).

IDEAS & INSPIRATION

Use this space to jot down your thoughts and ideas about Twitter.

_____

_____

_____

_____

Blogging with Blogger

Twitter and Google Reader are excellent ways to discover and consume information about homeschooling. Still, the ultimate commitment to connecting involves producing content of your own to share with others. The easiest way to do this is through blogging.

By blogging, you are sharing your ideas and experiences with the world. Just as you are now reading blogs of others, you can also contribute to the conversation. Whether you document the experiences and educational journey of your children, reflect on your life as a parent and teacher, or share ideas and resources, blogging can be incredibly satisfying and beneficial.

One of the most common things people say when we encourage them to blog is, "No one out there would want to read what I write." First of all, this isn't true! And second, how do you know if you don't try? Give it a shot!

Blogging is an opportunity to connect with the homeschooling world, give your children's work an audience, and contribute your voice to the discussion.

Blogger Essentials

We recommend using Google's blogging platform, Blogger, for its ease of use and accessibility.

Getting started

Go to www.blogger.com, sign in with your Google account, and click the "New Blog" button.

Give your blog a name and a URL. Use the "Check availability" link to make sure no one has claimed that address already. Choose a template (you can always change this later), then click "Create Blog."

Once you've created a blog, each time you log into www.blogger.com, you'll be taken to your "Dashboard," a central page showing all your blogs and featuring a menu of actions for each one.

Adjusting settings

Before making your first blog post, it's a good idea to adjust some settings. To do this, choose "Settings" from the drop-down menu on your dashboard.

Some settings you may want to adjust are "Basic," "Posts and Comments," "Phone and Email," and "Other."

In "Basic," you can grant permissions to other authors, decide who can read your blog, edit your blog's title, and add a description.

With the "Posts and Comments" settings sub-category, you can choose how many posts show on your main page, who can comment, enable comment moderation (so that no comments become public without your permission), and create a comment message (i.e., a note that appears when readers comment). If you're posting your children's work or having your children create their own blogs, it's a good idea to create a comment message that encourages positive, friendly comments.

In the "Phone and Email" settings sub-category, you can set your blog so that you can post from your phone or via email.

The "Other" setting sub-category can be used to delete your blog, if necessary.

Layout

Choosing "Layout" from the "More Options" dropdown menu will allow you to change the appearance of your blog and add helpful elements.

From the page that opens, you'll be able to insert many cool and helpful tools into your blog's sidebar by selecting "Add a Gadget." The most useful basic gadgets include:

- *Follow by Email:* Enables readers to subscribe to your blog via email.

- *Slideshow*: Embed class photos.

- *Poll*: Survey your readers with a multiple choice question.

- *Blog List*: Suggest blogs for students or parents to follow.

- *Blog Archive:* Access to all of your blog posts, arranged by month.

- *Search Box:* Allows users to search your blog.

- *Link List*: Provide students or parents with recommended websites or links to your other pages.

- *HTML/JavaScript*: Add code from other sites to embed a widget. (More on widgets, momentarily.)

Some notes on layout

- Choose "Template" from the menu in the left sidebar to change the look and design of your blog, including the blog's background. Blogger offers several template options, as well as the ability to customize your blog's appearance.

- Explore the other offerings, too. One favorite in the "Most Popular" category is the "Countdown" gadget. Make countdowns to projects, field trips, due dates, etc.

- In the layout screen, click the "Edit" link in any gadget's gray box to make changes or remove it.

- Want your Twitter updates to appear in your sidebar? Click "Add a Gadget" and choose "Featured." A Twitter gadget will be one of the options.

- Need to change the order of your gadgets in your sidebar? Simply drag and drop the gray rectangles in the sidebar to reorganize them. Be sure to click the orange "Save Arrangement" button after doing this.

Posting

You can make a new post from your dashboard (orange button). When you click the "New Post" button, you will be able to title and type your post.

If you are logged into Blogger, you can also publish a new post directly from your blog's home page by clicking "New Post" in the upper right hand corner.

Publishing a post is pretty straightforward. Just type your post into the text editor. Three important buttons are:

- *Link*: For making hyperlinks

- *Image*: From the web via URL or upload

- *Video*: Upload only, and must embed with HTML from web

Post settings

The Post Settings menu in the right sidebar offers some useful options, such as adding labels, scheduling your post, controlling comments, and more.

Labels

Labels help you organize your posts by topic. You can use as many labels as you'd like (e.g., a post about social studies homework could be labeled *social studies* and *homework*). You can even add a gadget to your sidebar that links to all your posts by label. Apply labels using the "Labels" link.

Schedule

Using the "Schedule" link, you can write blog posts in advance and schedule them to post on the date and time you want them to.

Disallow comments

If you want to remove the option of user comments on your individual post, do this in by clicking the "Options" link. (To disallow comments on all your blog posts use the Blog Settings. See *Adjusting settings* on page 17.)

Publish

When you're done posting, just click "Publish" (or "Save" if you want to come back to it later).

Edit or delete posts

From time to time you may need to edit or delete posts you've made. Do that by clicking "Posts" from the "More Options" dropdown menu in your Dashboard.

Email and RSS subscriptions

To make it easier for other parents and families to follow your blog, you'll want to set up subscription options for them. That way, every time you publish, they'll be notified automatically. You can use one of two methods to enable this.

Method One: Email Subscription with Feedburner

This process will allow you to add a gadget to your blog that people can use to set up an email subscription. They'll get an email that contains your new blog posts every time you submit one.

1. Choose "Layout" from the More Options drop down menu on your Dashboard.

2. Click "Add a Gadget."

3. Scroll down and select "Follow by Email."

4. Change the heading/title if you want, then click "Save."

Now anyone can subscribe to your blog via email. After entering their address, they'll be asked to type in a security code (to prevent spammers), and then they'll receive a confirmation email from Feedburner. This confirmation email will contain a link that they must click to activate the subscription.

If you're interested in learning more about your blog's subscribers or if you want to experiment with your feed settings, you can do so by logging in with your Google username at www.feedburner.com.

Method Two: RSS

Email is by far the easiest and most common way for people to subscribe to your blog. But there's also the option of adding an RSS (real simple syndication) subscription for tech-savvy readers who prefer to use RSS readers to read your blog.

Blogger has a gadget that allows readers to subscribe in an RSS reader. Here's how to add it to your sidebar:

1. Choose "Layout" from the "More Options" drop down menu on your Dashboard.

2. Click "Add a Gadget."

3. Scroll down and select "Subscription Links."

4. Change the heading/title if you want and click "Save."

This will now be seen on your sidebar allowing readers to subscribe using popular RSS readers.

Embedding

"Embedding" means to insert an object in an application, such as Blogger. To embed an object, be it a document, video, slideshow, or widget from a third party source, all you need to know how to do is copy and paste. As long as you put the code in the right place, this is very easy.

1. Start with a new post.

2. In a new tab or window, locate the object you want to embed. This can be a slideshow from SlideShare, a video from YouTube, Vimeo, or Animoto, a document from Scribd, a Voicethread, a Google Doc or Map, or any number of things.

3. Find that object's embed code—a long line of HTML—and copy it. Most sites will have a "share" or "embed" button to click.

4. Now go back to your blog post. Paste the HTML code directly into your blog post.

5. You can now re-insert your cursor and continue typing below the object, or you can publish. If you want to see what your post will look like with the embedded object prior to publishing, click the "Preview" button (next to "Save Now").

6. Once you've published, click "View Blog" to see your finished post.

The following sites offer popular content for educational blog embeds:

- *Scribd*: Upload documents to access and download through your blog.

- *Slideshare*: Upload PowerPoint presentations to embed in your blog.

- *YouTube, Vimeo, and Teacher Tube*: Videos galore!

- *Animoto*: Great for children's video projects or slideshows. (Learn more on page 46.)

- *Voicethread*: Create collaborative slideshows. (See page 33.)

- *Google Docs*

- *Google Maps*

If you ever find an embed code, you've found something that can be shared in your blog! Just remember to always cite your sources.

Embedding widgets in your sidebar

A widget is a small snippet of code that is also known as a gadget or badge. Blogger, as you now know, includes many gadgets, but other websites have them as well.

Just as a practice example try this activity: http://bit.ly/widgetpractice. The steps in this document will lead you through installing a weather widget on your blog.

Often, you'll discover cool third-party widgets on others' blogs. Usually, there will be a link somewhere on the widget, which you can click to get one just like it for your own blog.

Building your readership

A frequent concern we hear from beginning bloggers is, "But who in the world will read my blog?" We have a couple of responses to that question.

First, be sure that you're writing for yourself. Write about things that have meaning for you, things that are important and interesting to you. Don't worry about writing for others. If you're writing for yourself, you'll be able to reflect more deeply, and this is one of the best aspects of blogging. It allows us to ponder, contemplate, and reflect on our work. If you're writing about what interests you, it will also help you stay motivated to write regularly. There is no shortage of thoughts in your own mind! Don't worry about writing what others want to read. Write instead what you want to write.

That being said, it is definitely fun and rewarding to know that others are reading what you write, so be sure to promote each post. Use Twitter, Facebook, Google+, and any other social media network that you are a part of to promote your writing. This will generate readership and a subscriber base. Before you know it, readers will be retweeting and sharing your work with others.

IDEAS & INSPIRATION

Use this space to jot down your thoughts and ideas about Blogger and blogging.

_____

_____

_____

_____

_____

Social Bookmarking: Diigo

The final connection method we'll discuss is one of our favorites. It is also, in our opinion, one of the most under-utilized. It's called social bookmarking. Our social bookmarking tool of choice is Diigo.

What is social bookmarking? It is a means of bookmarking websites so that they are saved "in the cloud," meaning you can access them from any computer. Chances are you already utilize bookmarks through your web browser so that your favorite sites can be easily accessed when you need them. However, this makes it so your bookmarks are saved only on *your* computer. Also, this method makes it difficult to share your bookmarks with others. Social bookmarking fixes both of these problems, and it's incredibly easy to use.

In the following section, we'll show you how to get started with the social bookmarking site Diigo, including how to save and organize bookmarks, as well as how to use Diigo as a research tool, and how to connect with other Diigo users to easily share bookmarks.

Diigo Essentials

Getting started

Go to www.diigo.com and click on the "Join Diigo" button.

Once you have an account, it is important to make it easy to use. You need to install a bookmarklet (button) on your web browser's toolbar so that you can bookmark pages with one click of the mouse. To do this, click on the "Tools" button.

There are several options based on which browser you use. We would suggest using "Diigolet." Simply click on the link and drag the icon to your bookmark bar. Click on the new button and login using the information you just used when creating the account. When you click the "Diigolet," you will see a menu of options that includes a button labeled "Bookmark."

While you are still on the "Tools" page, you may want to consider the additional "Web Services." Probably the most important feature as you get started is "Import bookmarks," which will allow you to pull in your old bookmarks from nearly anywhere.

You're set up. Now what?

Now it's time to fully harness the power of Diigo. When explaining tagging, we like to use the metaphor of taking a picture of your children on Christmas. Where do you save the picture? Do you put it in a folder for both girls? Do you put it in a folder for Christmas? Do you make a folder for all pictures taken during that winter? There are so many choices, and no matter which choice you make, you have to struggle to find the picture later on when you actually want it. With tagging, this is no longer an issue.

For example, through your Google Reader, let's say you've used found an interesting webpage, such as the Engaging Educators home page. If you want to bookmark this page for future reference, should you put it in the PLN folder, homeschool folder, or EdTech folder? With Diigo, you tag it with all three, just by clicking on the "Diigolet" button, then "Bookmark," and then tagging it.

You have several options from this window. If you want to keep this bookmark for just yourself, be sure to check the "Private" box. If you want to be able to come back to this page even if the page is gone, you should click the "Cache" button. You have a limited number of pages that you can cache unless you use premium features. Of course, you can type a description in the "Description" box. Most important, you should type in as many tags as you need in the tags field, and make sure to separate them with a space. Finally, you can "Share to a Group," if you belong to a group. More on that soon.

Managing your tags

You're using Diigo. You're tagging sites. It's really easy. Now what? Since you have tagged sites, you can visit your Diigo page by using the following URL where "yourusername" is your user name: http://www.diigo.com/user/yourusername. You can see all of your bookmarks listed under the "My Library" button. Click on the tags to limit the pages that are shown.

The social aspect

Next to "My Library" is "My Network." These are people you follow or who follow you.

After "My Network" is "My Groups." These are groups that you belong to. You can also create a group. There are different levels of openness with groups, so check your settings carefully. For example, the educators group is pretty much open to anyone who wants to join. However, the EngagingEd group is by invite only because it is setup only for members of Engaging Educators to use.

The last feature that we want to share with you is the search window. By typing in the search window, you get several options. You can search your library for the tagged words. You can search the community, which is our personal favorite. We like this because it helps you sort through the billions of useless webpages. You can see how many people found different sites worth bookmarking. Finally you can search for users or groups that also match the keywords. This really does making social bookmarking social.

Additional features

From the "Diigolet" button, you can highlight and put sticky notes on pages, which will be saved. As we mentioned before, Diigo does have a great help page to assist you with what we didn't explain well or at all. Finally, if you are interested in ed tech, you may want to consider adding users twetherb and bcurran to your network. Also, feel free to follow our group EngagingEd.

IDEAS & INSPIRATION

Use this space to jot down your thoughts and ideas about bookmarking with Diigo.

_____

_____

_____

_____

_____

Collaborate

*C*onnecting with other homeschooling families can be exciting and inspirational. Once you make these connections, it will become easier to take part in an even more rewarding 21st century activity: collaboration.

Why should collaboration be a cornerstone of your homeschooling activities? It offers a chance for your children to participate in authentic learning activities. This includes working with others from around the world, sharing and discussing ideas, creating projects together, and more.

Through the connections that you've made with Twitter, blogs, and other social media networks, you can set up these opportunities for your children to collaborate. It can range from simple activities such as using Skype to discuss geography or a book that you are reading with another family in a different state to more complex projects such as collaboratively designing websites and multimedia projects.

Now is a great time to mention the concept of "global collaboration." This refers to projects worked on by children from different countries. If you ever had a pen pal as a kid, you know how exciting it can be to communicate with friends from another part of the world. In the 21st century, kids across the globe are able to not just connect and communicate with each other, but collaborate as well.

Using Twitter and blogs to find global collaborative partners can yield positive results. Online communities that have message boards, such as ePals (www.ePals.com) or the Gifted Homeschoolers Forum (www.giftedhomeschoolers.org/online-community/), can be useful for these efforts, as well.

Once you have people with whom you can collaborate, it's time to come up with a project. Trading letters or emails is fun, but your objective is thinking and learning, so be creative and go deeper with your collaborative activities.

We are going to share five tools you can use to collaborate along with brief descriptions about the types of collaborative work you can do with each.

Google Drive

This Google application, formerly known as Google Docs, is one of the easiest ways to digitally collaborate with others. All you need is a Google account. Google Drive functions as both an online hard drive, allowing you to upload all kinds of files, from documents to photos to videos, and as an online productivity suite (think of it as an online version of Microsoft Office). No matter how you use it, anything you upload to or create with Drive can be accessed from any computer with Internet access and shared with others.

Google Drive Essentials

Accessing Google Drive

Access Google Drive at http://drive.google.com. From there you'll see your Google Drive home page.

Creating documents

We'll start with the productivity suite. Drive enables you to create documents, spreadsheets, presentations, and more. Simply click the "Create" button and choose the type of item you want to make from the list.

Most frequently, we use Drive to create documents. When you create a document, you see what appears to be a simple word processing program, but there's much more to Google Drive than meets the eye. When you click the blue "Share" button in the upper right corner (or choose "Share" from the "File" menu), you'll be able to share it with people with whom you'd like to collaborate. Simply type their email addresses into the field in the Share window.

Collaborating

After you've done this, your collaborators will be notified via email. From their own Google Drive pages, they'll be able to access your document and collaboratively create, revise, and edit it with you *in real time*. Yes, you can share your documents and other Google Drive creations with as many people as possible, and you can simultaneously work on it together, but keep in mind that Documents and Spreadsheets have a limit of 50 live collaborators, at one time, while presentations have a limit of 10 live collaborators.

You will know other collaborators are viewing because their names will be displayed above the document. Each person's cursor will appear as a different color. Also, when others are viewing, you will see a note in the upper right portion of your screen showing how many are viewing. When you click that note, a chat window will open up, allowing you to chat in real time.

Leaving comments

Not all interactions need to be (or can be) simultaneous in Google Drive. The "Comments" feature can be used to leave notes for your collaborators when they aren't there in real time. There are two ways to do this:

1. To leave a comment about a specific part of the document or spreadsheet, highlight the text about which you're leaving a comment, then right-click (command+click on a Mac) and select "Comment." Now, when your collaborators view the document they will see this comment and will be able to reply to it or mark it "resolved." Each time a comment is posted, edited, or resolved, an email notification is sent to all the collaborators.

2. Click the "Comments" button in the upper right corner. This will open all of the active comments and allow you to leave a general comment for your collaborators.

When to Use Google Drive

Collaboration is a vital 21st century skill. Your children can practice it by connecting with kids in other locations and then using Google Docs to create a report, slideshow, data sheet, or scads of other ideas. When children are working together to build learning artifacts— tangible evidence of their learning—they are building authentic skills, skills they will use for years to come.

Here are five quick ideas for collaborative projects using Google Drive:

1. Gather weather data from around the world (each contributor shares temperature and/or precipitation from their location).

2. Present findings from a shared research topic via a shared document and/or presentation.

3. Write a story or poem together. Collaborators take turns adding lines to the story or poem.

4. Collaborate with a partner to practice peer-editing skills. Each writes a paragraph or essay, and the other edits it.

5. Collaborative note taking. Use a document as a place for storing notes for a common project or a shared essay or story.

IDEAS & INSPIRATION

Use this space to jot down your thoughts and ideas about Google Drive.

_____

_____

_____

_____

_____

Voicethread

Voicethread is a unique tool for creating multimedia slide shows—with a collaborative twist. Once the slideshow has been created, using images, documents, or video, viewers can navigate through the slides and leave comments in five different ways: via computer microphone, text, audio upload, webcam, or telephone (although with the last two, you get a limited number of minutes for free and then you're charged for additional minutes).

To explain it in another way, imagine creating a Powerpoint presentation that consisted of 10 slides, each with a question on it. Then imagine sending it to 10 of your friends and asking them to answer the questions by making an audio recording of their answers. With Voicethread, there's no "sending," just sharing a link or (even more simply) embedding the Voicethread within your blog, wiki (see page 36), or website. And, there's no confusion about how to record and attach answers or comments; it's all done with a couple of clicks.

Voicethread is a fun, engaging, and easy way to have a conversation around a set of images, documents, or videos. Its benefits lie in its interactive and collaborative experience. By enabling viewers to comment and interact with its contents, Voicethread brings an entirely new approach to what is normally a one-sided experience: viewing a slideshow.

Here's a quick overview of the steps required to create a Voicethread.

Voicethread Essentials

Get an account

The best way to do this is to get an educator's account via http://ed.voicethread.com. The free version of the educator's account limits you to a total of 50 free Voicethreads and limits your webcam and phone commenting to just a handful of minutes. Still, the free version is more than adequate for a homeschooling family.

Create a slideshow

Once you're logged in, click the "My Voice" link at the top of the ed.voicethread.com home page. You'll be taken to a dashboard that shows the Voicethreads you've created and allows you to browse through public Voicethreads that others have made. This is a great way to find some inspiration. Find the tab labeled "Create," which is where you start.

Once you've clicked the create tab, simply upload the images, documents, or videos of your choice, using the "Upload" button.

Comment and share

After you choose your content, your Voicethread will be created. You can then leave comments of your own by clicking on the second button. You can skip this part if you want, and go right to sharing. The "Share" button allows you to share the Voicethread you've just created via email (you can also generate a URL, or web address, to share). Once you click "Share," you'll see a menu asking you to decide if you want to allow anyone to comment or if you only want people to be able to view it. Other options include moderating comments, which sends you an email when anyone comments, and the comment will not appear on your Voicethread until you approve it. A final option is having your project appear on the Browse page, Voicethread's page of public projects that anyone can view.

In order to comment, the person viewing must first register for a free Voicethread account. They'll be prompted to do this when they click the "Comment" button on your Voicethread.

When to use Voicethread

Voicethread is a great option when you have a friend or family with whom you'd like to collaborate. You can take turns creating slideshows and leaving comments. Or, you could create a slideshow and send it to your entire network, asking them to comment and share their ideas. Remember, Voicethreads can include not just images but documents and videos, as well. The options are limitless.

Here are six ideas for simple Voicethread activities:

1. Post interesting images from sites such as PhotoPin.com or FlickrCC.bluemountains.net, or better yet, photos that you and your family have taken, and ask viewers to comment about what they notice. (These sites feature safe images that are licensed for reuse, so you don't have to worry about copyright.)

2. Analyze editorial cartoons or other primary sources by uploading them into a Voicethread and then have viewers comment with their analysis.

3. Add a series of images (use the above links for ideas) to create a story without words. Then have viewers add comments to create a digital "script."

4. Collaboratively edit and revise children's writing by uploading a part of a story they've written. Viewers can leave comments with revision suggestions, constructive criticism, and praise.

5. Use Voicethread as a more interactive alternative to PowerPoint. If you're thinking about making a PowerPoint presentation, use Voicethread instead and add narration via audio comment.

6. Document a science activity or field trip by uploading photos of the process or event. Then, add audio comments to create slides that explain the details of what's being shown in the photos.

IDEAS & INSPIRATION

Use this space to jot down your thoughts and ideas about using Voicethread.

_____

_____

_____

_____

_____

Wikispaces

Wikispaces.com is a site we hold close to our hearts. Wikis were one of our first attempts into the scary world of educational technology. It's not actually scary once you are in it, but when looking at it from the outside, it may seem quite intimidating.

What is a wiki? A wiki is a simple website that is easily edited and designed for collaboration. The people at Common Craft have made a fantastic three-and-a-half minute video that explains wikis very well. You can find that video by searching for "Common Craft wikis in plain English." A wiki with which you may be familiar is Wikipedia.

Why would you want to create a wiki? We'll get into specific ideas in a moment, but creating a wiki is a quick and easy way to make your own webpage. Even better, though, is the fact that it's a way of creating a webpage *collaboratively*.

There are several wiki websites, but Wikispaces is our favorite. Wikispaces is always improving, has tools designed for educators, and is very intuitive. You can have a wiki up and running in a matter of minutes.

Wikispaces Essentials

Getting started

Go to wikispaces.com. Make sure "Education" is selected at the top of the page, then click the "Teachers" button.

Click the "Sign up and start your wiki" button. You'll be prompted to create a username and password and to name your wiki (this can be changed later).

Edit button

Wikis, including Wikispaces, are designed around the edit button. Once you've logged into your account, your wiki will have an edit button. By clicking on that button your wiki acts like and has the same interface as a text document, basically turning your screen into what you'd see when typing something in Microsoft Word.

From this screen, you can enter, delete, and edit text.

Link

Use the "Link" button to insert hyperlinks to other wiki pages or to external web pages.

File

The "File" button allows you to insert files such as documents, spreadsheets, slide presentations, and images into your wiki page.

Widget

Clicking "Widget" opens a menu with a wide range of options, such as inserting videos from YouTube, chat boxes for live discussions between wiki-members, maps, tables of contents, calendars, and more.

Save

After you've finished editing, click the "Save" button and your page goes back to a normal webpage for the world to see.

Sidebar menu

One other menu on your wikispaces menu to know about is the sidebar menu. Use this menu to add pages to your wiki (use the plus sign) and manage the wiki (privacy settings, member permissions, look and feel, and more).

This is also the menu you use to invite users. What makes wikis extra special is that numerous people can be members of a wiki and have the rights to edit the wiki. This allows for collaboration from within the same room or around the world. Just click the plus sign next to "Members" and invite others to edit your wiki.

Privacy

The default setting of your wiki is "Private." This means only people you've given permission to edit the wiki can do so. It also means that ONLY members of the wiki can view it online. No one else will be able to see it, even if they go directly to the wiki page's address.

While this allows you strict control over what is published, it also takes away one of the most powerful and motivational aspects of publishing student work online: the global audience.

We recommend changing your wiki permissions to a "Protected" status. This allows anyone on the web to see your work, but ONLY approved members of the wiki can make edits. It's the best of both worlds. To change your privacy settings, choose "Manage Wiki" from the sidebar menu and select "Permissions."

Five ideas for Wikispaces activities

1. Create a simple, elegant eportfolio to document learning and allow people around the world to comment and celebrate.

2. Work with others, preferably from around the world, to collaboratively write and edit a story.

3. Create a dictionary or encyclopedia for a subject, topic, or project.

4. Use a wiki to create a project (see "Amazing Race" on page 61).

5. Collaborate with others to document something about your and their local areas, for example, water usage, climate, animal life, or current events.

IDEAS & INSPIRATION

Use this space to jot down your thoughts and ideas about using Wikispaces.

_____

_____

_____

_____

_____

Edmodo

A free social networking platform for students, Edmodo is a terrific way to connect, share, and collaborate with others. If you and your family have other families with whom you'd like to work, Edmodo is a great option. It's simple, safe, and free.

When people see the Edmodo interface for the first time, it often reminds them of Facebook, and in a way, it has many similarities. Users can post messages, share links and videos, and more. The most important difference, however, is that the parent has complete control over all aspects, and no one other than the people with whom you choose to connect ever have access to anything that is posted.

Edmodo works best when you have others with whom you want to connect. It doesn't have to be at a distance. It could be a connection next door, across the street, or across town. Once you've established your connection, you simply share a group code with your collaborators. Then, you'll all be able to join the same group.

Edmodo Essentials

Getting started

Go to Edmodo.com to sign up for an account. You'll do this as a "teacher." (The parent sign-up option is for parents of students in schools using Edmodo.) From there, you'll be taken to your Edmodo page.

Create a group

The interface is quite simple, and you'll even be given tips about "what to do now." If you are using Edmodo to collaborate with other families, the first thing you'll want to do is to create a group. This is how you'll be able to see each other's work and leave comments for each other, which is only possible when one of the parents has created a group for other parents and children to join.

To create a group, just click "Create" in the Groups box in the left sidebar. You'll be asked to name the group, select a grade, and select a subject area. You'll then be given the group code, which is a series of characters that others will need in order to join your group. The best thing to do is to copy the code and email it to the families with whom you'll be collaborating.

Student accounts

Once children have this group code, they can create their own accounts by going to Edmodo.com, clicking "I'm a student," and pasting in the code when prompted. Children cannot create an Edmodo account without a group code. Even if you're just using Edmodo within your own family, you will have to have a "teacher" account and create a group (or groups) for your family to join.

Additional Edmodo information

Taking time to explore Edmodo is certainly worth it. It has many features built in that enhance the collaborative experience, including the option of creating polls and quizzes for children, creating assignments that have to be "turned in" by children in the group, creating virtual badges that children can earn, and the option of creating a library of resources.

Edmodo is well known for its technical and customer support. If you do need assistance or can't figure out something, the help page (located at http://help.edmodo.com) is immensely valuable. It also features "Communities," groups oriented around a common topic (such as math, social studies, and others). You can join communities to collaborate with other educators at http://edmodo.com/communities.

Five Ways to Use Edmodo

1. Create an online book club. Several families can read the same book and then use an Edmodo group to "meet" and "discuss" what you've read.

2. Collaborate to write stories. Within the group, one person starts the story and collaborators add comments to build and expand it.

3. Use it as a "backchannel" to discuss other shared experiences such as field trips, educational videos, and more.

4. Use it as a safe and easy way to trade digital letters among children in different locations.

5. Share digital creations such as movies or podcasts or numerous other works with your group, so they can admire and comment. This is a great way to get peer feedback.

IDEAS & INSPIRATION

Use this space to jot down your thoughts and ideas about using Edmodo.

_____

_____

_____

_____

_____

Create

So many web tools and applications are available to enable students to create their own content. Students no longer have to be passive consumers of information, taking in facts and regurgitating them later. This may be how learning continues to take place in our standardized-test-driven public schools, but the idea of children actively learning, analyzing, and synthesizing complex information, and taking control of their own learning by creating their own content is one that certainly fits the ideals and philosophies of most homeschooling parents we know.

In this section, we will introduce you to several web tools well-suited for children to use, giving ideas and tips for each one. Our objective is to help you provide your child with a digital "toolkit." Much like a carpenter's toolkit, which allows a carpenter to create and build innumerable projects with different objects and materials, a digital toolkit enables children to create and build various digital projects. Once you and your child have developed a toolkit that contains several different web-based tools, projects become much more dynamic and meaningful, and children will view learning in a completely new way.

At the conclusion of this section, we will describe six projects that we have done with children using some of these tools. With this background and expertise, you'll soon be creating exciting projects on your own!

Part One: Creation Tools

Screencast-o-matic.com

"Screencasts" are recordings of your computer's screen, usually with an added audio component, typically the screencaster recording his or her voice. As a result, screencasts are excellent for developing speaking and listening skills. Screencast-o-matic.com makes creating screencasts incredibly easy and can even be done without registering for an account, although having an account gives you access to your videos after they're created. Without an account, your videos aren't stored and disappear if you don't download them when you're finished.

Screencast-o-matic Essentials

Getting started

1. Go to Screencast-o-matic.com.

2. Click the big, blue "Start recording" button. (You may be prompted to accept and allow the Java plug-in at this point, depending upon your Internet browser's settings.)

3. Drag and resize the recording area. Click the red record button to begin recording. (The menus at the bottom of the frame will allow you to adjust resolution, audio, and other settings.)

4. Click the "Done" button when you're finished.

5. Upload it directly to YouTube or Screencast-o-matic (requires registration) or download the movie to your hard drive.

Handy screencasting tips

Always write a script

Knowing what to say ahead of time is vital. The recording limit is 15 minutes, so there may not be time for lots of "uhs," "ums," and other verbal fillers.

Practice makes perfect

Rehearsing ahead of time is a great idea. This helps to make your narration sound more natural and less robotic.

Listen to other screencasts

So you know what to do—and not do. A simple search of YouTube for "screencast" will give you plenty of examples.

Ideas for Screencast-o-matic

When would you want children to create screencasts? Countless ideas come to mind. Here are a few screencasts you and your children could create:

1. Tutorials of websites or web applications

2. Narrated photo or art slideshows with a recorded presentation made with Google Docs.

3. Narrated virtual tours of faraway places with a recording of Google Maps or Google Earth.

4. Explanations of math problems and concepts.

Xtranormal.com

Although we only generally promote free websites, Xtranormal.com is a fantastic site even if it might cost you a few dollars. The site is free to use, but there are opportunities for upgrades with minimal fees, which we think you might be enticed to use.

Xtranormal defines itself as "Animated Movies Made Easy!" Xtranormal provides you the tools to turn a script for one or more "actors" into an animated movie. The script you enter as text comes to life as the animated actors recite their lines. But beyond being just the writer, you get to be the director. You can drag in the gestures you want your characters to use with given lines. You can also pick the camera angles used throughout the video. Finally, you have numerous options for changing characters, setting, and background noise.

Xtranormal is a captivating tool and a great way to show learning. The scriptwriting process is important because Xtranormal reads the words phonetically and the punctuation used. In order to have a script sound right, it needs to be spelled and punctuated correctly. Xtranormal is intuitive and only takes a few minutes to learn, but it is a tool that you'll find yourself coming back to again and again.

Animoto

Movie-making is an incredibly engaging experience and a unique showcase children's learning. The site Animoto.com makes movie creation easy and fun.

Animoto allows you to add images, video, text, and music. They'll put it all together into a movie for you.

Animoto Essentials

Getting started

1. Apply for an educator's account at animoto.com/education. An educator's account allows your videos to have no time limit; otherwise the limit for free accounts is only 30 seconds.

2. Once you're signed up and signed in, click the "Create video" button.

Making a movie

1. Choose a style (i.e., background and theme) for your video.

2. Upload images or videos from your hard drive or from your Facebook, Flickr, or other photo site account.

3. Choose music or add your own (or choose "none"). The speed of your presentation's transitions is dependent upon your music's tempo. If you choose a slow song, the images will transition more slowly.

4. Decide if you want to spotlight any images. When you spotlight an image, Animoto will focus on that image longer than it focuses on images that aren't spotlighted. Spotlighted images show for about twice as long as non-spotlighted images.

5. Add text into any spot of your movie.

6. Produce the video. This can take a little time to happen, but Animoto will email you when it's done. You'll then be able to share the link or embed the video on a blog or website.

Ideas for Animoto

1. Make a book trailer to "advertise" a favorite book.

2. Create a public service announcement about a local or global social issue.

3. Use it as a fun alternative to photo slideshows. For example, showcase photos taken on a field trip.

4. Write a story and then use Animoto to tell the story "digitally," with images and text.

Prezi.com

PowerPoint revolutionized presentations. It's a wonderful tool, but it has a time and a place. As the 21st century powers on, the tools keep improving. We're in no way saying that Prezi should or could replace PowerPoint, but it is a powerful alternative with many features that PowerPoint can't match.

Prezi claims that it is "The Zooming Presentation," and we couldn't agree more. Prezi allows you to zoom around a large canvas sequentially or in any order needed. Prezi also allows you to zoom in or out. This creates an amazing effect. A word, image, or video can be so small that you can't even see it until the presentation zooms in. For example, let's say you have a picture of a lion and are discussing how it eats. Upon clicking the button, your Prezi zooms in on the lion's tooth, and as you're zooming in, you begin to see an image on the tooth. As the zooming process completes, the image is actually a full screen video that shows how lions hunt and eat.

Prezi is an incredibly powerful tool that is hard to explain in just words. That's why it's so great. Prezi.com does have wonderful tutorial videos that can be found at http://prezi.com/learn/. Next time you are planning a presentation, give Prezi a shot. You'll be surprised to see your presentation zoom to the next level with this new tool.

Edu.glogster.com

One great aspect of digital creation tools is the fact that they empower children to showcase their creativity. Creativity is critical to children's development, and the sky's the limit with these tools.

Glogster allows children to design and create to their hearts' content, using digital, multimedia posters. These posters, referred to as "glogs" (graphics blogs), can feature text, audio, images, and videos.

Glogster Essentials

Getting started

1. Sign up at edu.glogster.com.

2. Click "Create New Glog" button.

3. On the Glogster interface, choose "Wall" from the menu to change the background of the Glog and of the page (the visible part of the screen around the Glog).

4. Choose "Graphics" to add art and animations.

5. Choose "Text" to add text to your Glog. You'll be able to select the font and the style.

6. Choose "Image" to add photos. These can be images you upload or provide a web link for. (Grabbing an image with your webcam is only available to premium users.) Once you choose an image, you'll also be able to select the border.

7. Choose "Video" to add a video from your hard drive or the web. Users can also select the style of border (called a "player") that appears around the video.

8. You can save your work and return to it later or, if you're finished, click "Save & Publish" to publish your Glog. Now you can make it available for public viewing, embed it in a blog, or share it via email. Just click "Save & Publish." (You can also save your work and return to it later to finish.)

9. The "Data" and "Draw" buttons are only available to premium users.

Ideas for Glogster

1. Make an interactive poster about a book, movie, or poem.

2. Create a multimedia alternative to a persuasive essay about a social issue.

3. Use as an alternative to a research report.

4. Build an interactive biography of a famous person by creating a Glog.

5. Use to demonstrate and illustrate a science concept.

IDEAS & INSPIRATION

Use this space to jot down your thoughts and ideas about Creation Tools.

_____

_____

_____

_____

_____

Part Two: Ready-Made Projects

When you are getting your feet wet with 21st century tools and projects, a good amount of structure is recommended. In your first explorations, it's a good idea to follow some of our projects, or tweak them only slightly to meet your needs.

As you and your children become more comfortable with digital learning, consider easing up on the reins a bit and giving your children control over their own learning. Let them choose which tools they use, what they learn about, and what the final product is going to look like. Giving them freedom to explore, discover, and create brings amazing results. Best of all, your children will be more engaged learners.

Project-Based Learning

Project-Based Learning (PBL) is an increasingly popular learning method in which children learn through the completion of projects focused on a central question, called "the driving question." Children work independently toward answering that question.

Example driving questions include:

- Is China a superpower?

- How should our town improve its mass transit system?

- How could you get more children interested in art museums?

- Should the American military intervene in humanitarian crises?

- Is it better to buy or lease a car?

PBL is more than just assigning kids to create a poster or a diorama: it involves deep and meaningful work around questions that are rich, engaging, cross-disciplinary, and open-ended.

Once you are comfortable with some of the tools and projects we recommend in this section, consider diving deeper into the world of PBL. One of the best Project Based Learning resources on the web is the Buck Institute for Education, www.bie.org.

Blogging

As we discussed earlier (see *Subscribing to Blogs with Google Reader*, page 2), blogs are an excellent source of reading material. Even more, publishing children's writing in blogs can be highly motivating.

Having children blog has many benefits. Some of these are:

Global audience

Children become inspired to write great things when they realize that their words can be read by people from all over the world.

They also become more attentive to details such as spelling, grammar, punctuation, and all the other things that often slip through the cracks when children aren't highly motivated to write.

Creative outlet

Blogs can be custom designed to match a blogger's personality. Also, blog posts can include rich and diverse multimedia, from embedded surveys to images to relevant videos.

Social media experience

Yes, blogs are considered "social media." This is because readers can interact with the writer by leaving comments. Learning how to write responsibly and respond appropriately to comments is critical. Children will no doubt be using social media increasingly as they get older. Helping them practice good "netiquette" and Internet safety will result in positive habits as they become more active on sites like Facebook, Twitter, and whatever else will be invented as they grow up.

Positive digital footprint

Imagine the power of your child being able to share the blog that she's been writing for several years with college recruiters or at job interviews. Imagine that same recruiter or interviewer searches for your child's name, only to discover a collection of powerful, reflective writing. In the 21st century, these situations are a reality. Helping children to not only understand this, but to seize this opportunity to make a quality impression, is critical.

Record of learning

If a child blogs regularly over an extended period of time, his blog can serve as a tremendous record of his growth. Imagine if a seven-year-old began blogging, and continued to do so once a week until the age of 16. Even if this involved creating different blogs along the way, this would serve as a permanent archive and remarkable opportunity to demonstrate how he has learned and grown over time.

Blog Ideas

Your children could start blogs for an infinite number of purposes. They could write one about a specific topic or perhaps several topics over time. Either way, the benefits are numerous.

What should your children blog about? The answer is simple: anything they want! We believe that when children are put in charge of their learning, when they are given choices about what and how they learn, they become more motivated and high-achieving.

Nevertheless, we have worked with children blogging on several occasions and helped them start blogs for various projects. Here are four blogging ideas that might help you come up with blogging projects for your own children.

Social justice blogs

After exploring global issues, children can reflect and share what they have learned and what they believe.

Reading reflection blogs

An easy way to get blogging is to write about and review books (or movies or games or anything, for that matter).

Experience blogs

Taking a field trip? Blog about it. Family vacation? Blog about it. Nature walk? You get the picture. Everything you and your children do has the potential to lead to a learning experience. Each time this happens, write about it and share it with the world. Don't forget to include photos!

Informational blogs

Another simple way to get blogging is to write about what you're learning. Whether this involves writing about people, places, current events or history, or even the theme of "What I Learned

Today," it's an easy way to get your children writing about their learning experiences.

Privacy

We believe Blogger is a great option (see *Blogging with Blogger*, page 16). Keep in mind that while Blogger does allow you to change settings that restrict comments and visibility, unless you make these changes manually, any blog you create will be visible (and searchable) on the web.

If you would like a blogging platform with more control in regards to privacy settings, we recommend KidBlog.org.

Promoting

One thing that can be very exciting for children is when people comment on their blogs. In order for this to happen, you have to sometimes put in a little work. Don't be shy to use Twitter to promote your kids' blogs. Tweet a link each time they make a post and the chances of receiving comments goes up dramatically. Increase the odds even more by using the #homeschool hashtag or the hashtag that was created specifically for soliciting blog comments: #comments4kids.

IDEAS & INSPIRATION

Use this space to jot down your thoughts and ideas about blogging projects.

_____

_____

_____

_____

_____

Google Maps

Google Maps (http://maps.google.com) is an incredibly useful web tool that enables children to learn, create, and explore. Google Maps users can create interactive maps of locations anywhere in the world. This is great to do if you're visiting a city on vacation and would like to map out the restaurants and sights you want to visit. We have also had a lot of success using Google Maps as a learning tool for children.

On a basic level, Google Maps is an engaging way for children to explore places both near and far. A simple search for a city or landmark transports users "into the map." Google Maps integrates images, first-person reviews from other users, and the ability to zoom to "Street View," so you can be virtually transported to that exact spot.

Street View is an amazing feature, one your children will find fascinating. To activate it on your Google Map, locate the yellow human figure on the zoom tool. Simply drag this figure onto the map to zoom to Street View at that location.

Another great feature of Google Maps is the ability to create your own personalized maps. Children might like do this for many reasons, and we'll give you a list of them shortly.

Google Maps Essentials

Getting started

1. Sign in to Google Maps with your Google account.

2. Search for any place in the world (such as Yellowstone National Park).

3. When it appears on the map, click on its placemark (the red icon that looks like a pushpin) and select "Save to Map."

4. From the drop down menu that appears, choose the map you want to save this location to (or choose "Create a new map...").

Once you've created your own maps, you'll be able to view them by clicking the "My Places" button on the top of the Google Maps home page. They'll appear in a list in the left sidebar. Just click on the one you want to see and it will open.

Google Maps Project

There is much more you can do with a personalized map, though. You can change the placemarks, add text, images, videos, and more.

Here's a project idea that we like to use when kids are reading a book that takes place in different settings, such as *The Maze of Bones* by Rick Riordan, *Walk Two Moons* by Sharon Creech, or *The Grapes of Wrath* by John Steinbeck: Create a map that documents the different places that characters go in the book.

For example, in *Walk Two Moons*, the main character travels across the country with her grandparents, stopping in places that are relevant to her family history. Children could create a Google Map that tracks this journey. You can provide them with writing prompts or thought-provoking questions for each stop along the way and they can add their writing to the map. With one group, we asked kids to write a postcard from each place from the main character's point of view to explore her feelings at each point in the story.

Adding notes

1. Open your map by clicking on "My Places," and then on the map name.

2. Click the edit button at the top of the left sidebar. Once you've done that, clicking on any of the place names in the sidebar will open the placemark with a text box for adding text. Just type it in,

and click "OK." From then on you'll be able to see the writing that has been added when you click on that place in your map.

Adding images and videos

Children also enjoy adding multimedia to their maps by changing the placemarks from the default bubbles into digital images or by embedding YouTube videos.

To add images, follow the steps above for editing a map. After clicking on a place name, click the placemark icon (it looks like a push-pin). This will enable you to change the icon to another of Google's options, or to add an icon of your own by uploading either a digital image that you or your child have taken or a photo you've downloaded from a photo sharing site such as PhotoPin.com or FlickrCC (http://flickrcc.bluemountains.net).

To add a YouTube video, copy the embed code from a YouTube video page (click "Share" to access it). Then, back on your map, follow the instructions for editing a placemark. In the window that opens, click "Edit HTML." Finally, paste in the YouTube embed code and your video will appear when you click that place on your map!

Google Maps Ideas

Here are some other ways Google Maps can engage children in meaningful learning:

Integrate math with the Google Maps measurement tool

You can use the Google Maps measurement tool to measure the distance between places on a map. To activate this feature, click on "Maps Labs" in the bottom of the left-side panel, then enable the "Distance Measurement" tool. Going forward, a little ruler icon will appear on your maps next to the map scale. Click that icon and you'll be able to click on any two points on your map to see the distance between them.

An alternative to a geography research report

Children can create a virtual field trip using interactive placemarks about important places in a country, region, state, or city. This can be done with places both far and near. An exploration of the history of your hometown is an exciting experience for kids and a Google Map adds a great deal to a project like this.

Explore current events

Each time you read a news story, you could create a new placemark and add an image, videos, or links to the original sources. Add a written summary of the event in the text box to create a highly interactive, multimedia representation of authentic learning.

Document learning on your family's field trips

Every time you travel to a museum, park, nature center, etc. create a new placemark that includes a photo your children took there, a written response about what they learned, and even a video they created on the trip and uploaded to YouTube.

Collaborate

Like Google Docs, multiple users can edit a Google Map. To share a map you've created with others, just click the "Collaborate" link in the left sidebar. You'll be given the option of inviting others to collaborate via email. Once you send this invite, they'll be able to edit this map and add placemarks to it, too. You can also make your map public for anyone to edit by checking the "Allow anyone to edit this map" box after you click the "Collaborate" link. This can be a cool thing to do when you're trying to create a map with a lot of other people. One such map was started by a teacher in Asia whose students wanted to know what the weather was like in different parts of the world. By enabling public editing, they were able to connect with and learn from students on three other continents! All it took was for the teacher to set the map to allow public editing and then sending out a link to the map via Twitter!

Share your maps on your blog

We've already talked about how kids can create blogs (see page 16). Google Maps makes it simple to embed a map into a blog or other website. Simply open your map and click the link button. This will open a box with the link to the map and the code for embedding the map. When embedded, your map is still completely interactive. Viewers can zoom, click, and open placemarks.

There are certainly many other educational uses of Google Maps. Once you get started, you're sure to think of many of your own!

IDEAS & INSPIRATION

Use this space to jot down your thoughts and ideas about projects with Google Maps.

_____

_____

_____

_____

_____

4-Icon Challenge

The 4-Icon Challenge is a project idea inspired by a blog post from a fellow Michigander, Ben Rimes (http://techsavvyed.net). The premise is simple: choose four images to represent the fundamentals of a story. This is done using photo sharing sites such as PhotoPin.com and FlickrCC (http://flickrcc.bluemountains.net).

While this may seem like a simple assignment, the challenge lies in digging deep and exploring the story's messages, themes, symbols, and other elements that lie beyond the text. These are important literacy skills, and this assignment is well suited for that.

For example, in a basic story like *The 3 Little Pigs*, a surface-level 4-Icon creation would be a picture of a pig, a wolf, a house, and a door. Yet, a child that explores this story on a deeper level might choose pictures that represent fear, naiveté, intelligence, over-confidence, or forethought.

This exercise can work well with any book or story. We've had some of our best results using books that have complicated plots and complex themes. For example, *A Wrinkle in Time* by Madeleine L'Engle turned out some terrific representations. Some students found images that showed love, friendship, family, and the complexities of human intellect. Other children focused on the conflict between good and evil or between reason and emotion.

One way we emphasize the "challenge" aspect of this assignment is to push kids to think of images that would be surprising and make someone say, "I never would have thought of that." Encouraging students to do more than simply retell the story with images is important, too. We push them to "dig deep" and try to represent a story's messages, rather than just its plot. Finally, we encourage children who do this project to explain their thinking through writing about their image choices. This adds written expression to a challenging thinking project.

Here are some ways that you could have students display the results of their 4-Icon Challenge work online:

Add four images to a blog post

This is easy to do and makes it very easy to add the written element.

Insert the four images into a Google Document

This also allows you to add text easily and adds a collaborative element: others who are reading the same story could add their four icons and written explanations to the document.

This project could also be adapted for social studies (find images to represent an historical event or geographic location) and science (find images that represent the impact of an invention or scientific discovery).

IDEAS & INSPIRATION

Use this space to jot down your thoughts and ideas about the 4-Icon Challenge.

_____

_____

_____

_____

_____

Amazing Race

The Amazing Race Project is something we've been running with kids and modifying for nearly 10 years. It is based on the CBS television show, *The Amazing Race*. In the original version of the project, which worked very well, children competed in an Amazing Race based on the educational content we wanted them to learn. Over time, the children began to develop the clues and create their own version of the Amazing Race. They then swapped their Amazing Race with other children and each group of children completed the other group's challenge.

We always start a project with a hook to grab the children's attention and to motivate them. Clips of *The Amazing Race* can be found at CBS.com and on YouTube.com. Carefully selecting the video clips you show can lead to great discussions and teachable moments.

We also include a couple of features based on the television show to help make the project more entertaining. One feature we have used is The Roadblock, which for us is a clue involving some kind of physical challenge for one member of the group. A clue we might ask would be, "The Mackinac Bridge is 26,371 feet long. How many minutes would it take you to walk across it?" We would then provide students with a tape measure and a stopwatch. They would have to measure the distance from the front door of the house to the mailbox and time how long it takes to walk there. Let's say the mailbox is 100 feet from the door and it takes 30 seconds to walk there. The children would have to figure out to divide 26,371 feet by 100 feet, then multiply that by 30 seconds, and finally, divide that by 60 seconds per minute to find out that it would take 131 minutes to walk across the bridge at the given speed. Once they solved this, they are given the next clue.

The second kind of special clue we use is The Detour, in which children are given a choice between two clues. The choice usually involves a rhyme or pun, but provides only minimal detail about what the clue will entail. A clue might be Chalk or Guac, as in guacamole. If the children chose the Chalk clue, they received "Find a piece of chalk and black construction paper in the house. On the black paper write in chalk how many miles it is from our house to Chalk River, Ontario." They would then use the computer, perhaps Google Maps, to find the answer. If the children chose the clue for Guac they received "According to the California Avocado Festival, how many years ago did the avocado originate?" (This clue involves understanding BC versus AD, which may make it more difficult.) This answer could be found through a Google search for "California Avocado Festival," navigating the website, and doing some simple math.

Children continue to complete these clues until they reach the end and win the race. If you want to add even more variety to your Amazing Race Project, you can find out much more about *The Amazing Race* at http://en.wikipedia.org/wiki/The_Amazing_Race.

IDEAS & INSPIRATION

Use this space to jot down your thoughts and ideas about the Amazing Race.

_____

_____

_____

_____

_____

Videos

A few years ago video creation was much more difficult than it is today. With the prevalence of cell phones, particularly smartphones, most people now carry video recorders in their pocket. Furthermore, many still cameras now shoot relatively high quality video. Once the videos have been shot, there are several tools you can use to put all the pieces together into a polished final product. Mac users can use iMovie (pre-installed on your Mac computer), while PC users can use Windows Movie Maker (pre-installed on your Windows machine) or Serif MoviePlus (software available for purchase at http://www.serif.com). All of these products work similarly and are relatively quick to learn. As a side note, be aware that iMovie has many advanced tools that need to be turned on. These tools allow for nice green screen use, picture-in-picture, and many other useful effects.

Videos typically fall into two, not mutually exclusive, categories. One category of video contains a series of still images while the other category contains a motion picture or series of motion pictures combined into a final video. Text, music, and transitions can be used to create a more polished final piece.

Video Project Ideas

Paint a picture of poetry with more than just words

Find or make images that represent a poem. Or, you can switch it up by writing poetry about images you've found. Add a title, some music, maybe the words to the poem, and you've got a polished piece.

Write and record a short script to create readers' theater

A few props, plus credits at the end, go a long way.

Create a book recommendation

Inspiration for this can be found at the end of each *Reading Rainbow* episode. These clips can be found at many local libraries or by searching YouTube for "reading rainbow book review." To give these videos a truly authentic *Reading Rainbow* feel, you can film them in front of a green screen. Any green butcher paper or green fabric will work. You can then add images or drawings from the book as the background for the video. A simple but really cool effect.

Describe a complicated concept in "plain English"

This idea is modeled after the videos produced by the company Common Craft (www.commoncraft.com). They make simple videos explaining topics that vary from the Electoral College to CFL light bulbs to website cookies. They do this by positioning a camera above a white table where a pair of hands moves words and drawings onto the screen to match the narration. We have had students create videos that explain different parts of speech in "plain English." This is a great way for them to demonstrate their learning and share it with others.

Define a word through video

Pick a word or phrase such as "life, liberty, and the pursuit of happiness." Find or create pictures that represent your choice. Explain what the word or phrase means in your own words and how the images reflect that. Put all of this together to create a nice video definition.

Children-created math tutorials

Examples of these can be found at http://mathtrain.tv/. These videos can be created in a variety of ways. Screen capture tools, such as Screencast-o-matic (see page 44), can be used to record videos of your computer screen. A second way would be to create a series of pictures or images explaining the topic. These images could be computer or hand drawn and scanned in. A simple narration of the images would complete this video. A third way would be to use live action, with the children performing on camera utilizing whiteboards, manipulatives, or markers and paper to illustrate a math topic. Keep a collection of these to document learning or work together to create a video math tutorial library.

Video creation is fun, easy, and educational. Nearly any project can be turned into, or at least include, a video. YouTube is a great resource. Create your own YouTube channel to upload your videos. With simple embedding, you can include your videos on nearly any website and let YouTube do all the hard work for you. Start small, and before you know it, you'll be shooting full length feature films—well almost.

IDEAS & INSPIRATION

Use this space to jot down your thoughts and ideas about digital video creation.

_____

_____

_____

_____

_____

Podcasting

Podcasting is one of our favorite projects because they're educational, creative, and simple. When creating a podcast project always follow the same steps:

Start with the end in mind

What objectives are you trying to meet with the project? Objectives can be both educational (e.g., understand the reasons for the colonies declaring independence) and developmental (e.g., be able to produce a project without assistance or publish work online).

Write a script

We *always* require children to write a script first. We do this for several reasons. First it provides an opportunity for children to practice writing. Second, it allows for discussion prior to creating the podcast. Third, it makes the podcasting process run much more smoothly. Fourth, many times it is nice to display the text with the recording.

Record the podcast

Don't worry about anything but recording the text. We recommend recording with many short tracks. This allows for easier editing later on and prevents a mistake ruining a whole recording. Continue recording and revising the podcast until the text sounds the way you want.

Publish the podcast

Add it to your blog or eportfolio. Tweet about it for others to check out. The work is a lot more fun when there is an audience.

Over the past years we've probably done hundreds of small and large podcast projects. Just about any project, paper, or idea can be podcasted.

Podcast Project Ideas

1. Create a radio talk show discussing a topic of your choosing.

2. Create a commercial selling a book, colony, country, etc.

3. Hold a pretend interview of an historic figure, a fictional character, etc.

4. Record a story you've written.

5. Record a collection of poems you've written.

6. Create an audio journal as an historical figure, a fictional character, etc.

7. Record a 60-second science report.

8. Create an audio reflection on your learning for the past however many days.

9. Create a radio game show in the style of Jeopardy!®.

10. Record a newscast about current events.

Collaborating and Sharing

If you collaborate with others, you will be amazed at the collection of project ideas your group will create. Sharing the creative load makes everything easier and encourages a more diverse range of projects. Don't forget to add the "phat" beats (i.e., amazing music). They really do polish up the project, as long as you don't take them too far. Finally, put it in your blog or wiki. You could also create your own podcast page with a site like Podbean (www.podbean.com), which makes it super easy to get your podcast available to the masses by adding it to the iTunes store for you! That authentic audience is priceless.

So, how to bring this to life? There are many options:

1. The easiest methods are with web-based services. These allow you to record audio via their website and then either download it or embed it in your blog. Good sites for this include Vocaroo.com and Audioboo.fm.

2. If you're an Apple user, you can easily record audio using GarageBand (factory-installed on your Mac or iPad) and Voice Memos (pre-loaded on your iPod Touch). Both options allow for easy conversion to MP3 audio, which is easily shared via your blog or via a podcast hosting site, such as podbean.com. GarageBand also offers the added bonus of integrated music "loops," which allows children to experiment with background music.

3. If you have a PC, you can download a free program called Audacity (http://audacity.sourceforge.net/) to record audio.

4. With your Google account, you have access to Google Voice (http://voice.google.com). Google Voice enables you to create your own online phone number with an online voicemail inbox. You simply call your number, make a recording, and then Google Voice allows you to download the recording as an MP3 or embed it in a wiki or blog. Essentially, using Google Voice allows you to podcast from your cell phone.

5. Finally, there's BlogTalkRadio.com, an online service that allows you to create your own "online radio show," complete with call-in guests! You schedule a show, call in as the host, and BlogTalkRadio automatically records your show and provides you with links and embed codes afterwards. (The free version is a little heavy on the ads, but not for anything inappropriate.)

IDEAS & INSPIRATION

Use this space to jot down your thoughts and ideas about podcasting.

_____

_____

_____

_____

_____

Digital Portfolios

While this idea may not technically qualify as a "project," we think it represents the peak of digital creation. We are speaking of the creation of a digital portfolio.

A digital portfolio is a collection of a person's best "learning artifacts" from a wide range of subject areas. In the 20th century, a portfolio collection would consist of handwritten or typed essays, worksheets, tests, and other papers filed in a folder. However, in the 21st century, things become much more exciting.

While a 21st century portfolio still represents a child's best work, it now exists completely in digital form.

Creating a Digital Portfolio

Build a "home base"

This will be where the portfolio is "stored." We suggest a wiki page that you can easily build with Wikispaces (see page 36). You can create a home page that features a photo and biography of your child. Then, you could add a page for each year of their educational life. You and your child can then fill each page with brilliant examples of learning. Just imagine what the finished product would look like at age 18!

Choose content

Obviously, you can't put everything in the portfolio. It would become too massive and unwieldy. Selectivity is key—but how to decide? We believe the decision-making should be split evenly between parent and child, with each choosing a few examples from each subject per year. The portfolio then becomes a collection of work of which both parent and child are proud.

Because it's a digital portfolio, it can contain all different types of learning activities. All of the tools and projects we've described in the Create section offer the option of creating a web address (URL) that links directly to the product. Most also offer the option of embedding the content directly into the wiki page. This is especially useful because viewers do not have to click out of the portfolio to view the work. When it's embedded, it can be viewed directly from the webpage.

Reflect

One critical aspect of portfolios that is often overlooked is reflection. For each piece collected in the portfolio, the child should create some sort of reflection as a way of assessing his or her own work. A portfolio reflection does not have to be anything too complicated, but it should involve your child answering reflective questions such as:

- What did I learn?

- What did I do best?

- What could I have done better?

- What surprised me about my work?

- What did I learn about learning?

Obviously, this is far from a complete list. Feel free to expand on these questions or to think of your own. What's important is that learners look back on a regular basis to ponder their own work and their growth.

There are many different options for capturing these reflections, too. Handwritten work could be scanned or photographed and then added to the wiki. (We like to put the reflections directly below the learning artifact on the wiki page.) Reflections could also be made via audio or video recording.

IDEAS & INSPIRATION

Use this space to jot down your thoughts and ideas about digital portfolios.

_____

_____

_____

_____

_____

Conclusion

Chances are, your homeschooling experience is energetic, engaging, and exciting. It's also probably filled with exploration, discovery, and creativity. You value all of these things, and your passion and love for your kids drives you to keep improving.

A 21st century homeschool is filled with all of these things and more. It's connected to other homeschool families via blogs, Twitter, and other social media, such as Diigo. It's collaborative. Twenty-first century homeschools do not function in isolation: they learn and explore with others, whether those people are across the dining room table, across the street, across the country, or even across the world. Finally, a 21st century homeschool is a place where children are empowered to create digital artifacts, and to share these with the world as evidence of their learning. Expecting children to sit and passively consume information, regurgitating it on command, is *so* last century. We have at our disposal a vast assortment of free and easy-to-use tools that put children in the driver's seat, where they can learn and discover just about anything.

As the digital age progresses, it is becoming increasingly clear that integrating technology into our children's education is less of an option and more of a necessity. Luckily, your passion for teaching your children and helping them in any and every way possible will make these changes to your approach more effective and easy.

So, why aren't all parents connecting, collaborating, and creating with their children?

For some it's a daunting task. Too many new things, too much to learn, too much unknown. If you're a member of this group, we recommend baby steps. Remember, don't try to take on all of these concepts and ideas at once. Add one at a time. Proceed slowly. Don't be afraid to fail, and when you do, be sure to try again.

As lifelong learners ourselves, we've failed countless times along the way. And we continue to fail as we try new things. This doesn't mean we don't keep trying new things. Every failed attempt is a learning opportunity. In short, when it comes to technology and education, be the type of learner you want your children to be—a learner that is dedicated, motivated, not afraid to try new things, and one who recognizes the immense value of learning from mistakes.

For other parents, an element of fear still exists. They fear the Internet and all that their children might be exposed to. It is natural to want to protect our children; however, it's also important to remain rational. Using technology with young children is great practice for them and a great way to teach them to be safe on the web. We wouldn't recommend any sites that we wouldn't use with our own kids, and we certainly don't recommend collaborating with anyone about whom you're unsure. There are teachable moments about online behavior everywhere you turn. Don't let fear prevent you from providing your children with meaningful learning experiences. (Check out our Internet Safety page for tips and resources: http://bit.ly/homeschoolnetsafety.)

You chose to teach your children at home for an incredibly important reason: their well-being and their learning mean the world to you. We hope this book has inspired you to shift the teaching and learning in your home to include the essential 21st century skills of connecting, collaborating, and creating. Enjoy the journey!

Appendix

In this appendix, you will find listings of useful websites, URLs, and tweeters to help your homeschool *connect, collaborate, and create.*

<u>Internet Safety</u>

Internet Safety Workshop
    http://bit.ly/homeschoolnetsafety

17 Cartoon Videos Explaining the Internet and Internet Safety to Kids
    http://www.freetech4teachers.com/2013/01/17-cartoon-videos-explaining-internet.html#.UOjSFuRTySp

<u>Blogs to Follow</u>

Gifted Homeschoolers Forum Blogroll
    http://giftedhomeschoolers.org/blogs/

Wonderopolis
    http://wonderopolis.org

The Kid Should See This
    http://thekidshouldseethis.com

The New York Times Learning Network
    http://learning.blogs.nytimes.com/

CNN Student News
    http://cnnstudentnews.blogs.cnn.com/

PBS News Hour Extra
  http://www.pbs.org/newshour/extra/

All the blogs at How Stuff Works
  http://blogs.howstuffworks.com/

Scientific American podcasts
  http://www.scientificamerican.com/podcast/

Homeschool Blog Bundle
  http://bit.ly/homeschoolblogs

Tech Savvy Ed
  http://techsavvyed.net

Blogging Tools

Blogger
  www.blogger.com

Feedburner
  www.feedburner.com

Google Reader
  www.google.com/reader

KidBlog.org
  http://bit.ly/widgetpractice

Gifted Homeschoolers Forum Blogging Group
  https://www.facebook.com/groups/bloggiingGHF/

Collaboration

Google Drive
  http://drive.google.com

Voicethread
  http://ed.voicethread.com

Edmodo
  http://edmodo.com

Wikispaces
  http://wikispaces.com

Forums

ePals
www.epals.com

Gifted Homeschoolers Forum
www.giftedhomeschoolers.org/online-community/

Photo Sites

FlickrCC
http://flickrCC.bluemountains.net

PhotoPin
http://photopin.com

Podcasting

Audioboo
http://audioboo.fm

Blog Talk Radio
http://blogtalkradio.com

Audacity
http://audacity.sourceforge.net/

Podbean
http://podbean.com

Vacaroo
http://vocaroo.com

Presentation

Animoto
http://animoto.com/education

Glogster
Edu.glogster.com

Google Maps
http://maps.google.com

Prezi
http://prezi.com

Screencast-o-mastic
http://screencast-o-matic.com

Xtranormal
http://xtranormal.com

Project-based Learning

Buck Institute for Education
www.bie.org

Engaging Educators
http://www.engagingeducators.com/project-birth.html

Social Bookmarking

Diigo
www.diigo.com

Diigo Groups
http://groups.diigo.com/group/engaginged
http://www.diigo.com/user/bcurran
http://www.diigo.com/user/twetherb

Twitter

Twitter
www.twitter.com

HootSuite tutorial
http://bit.ly/hootsuitebasics

HootSuite
www.hootsuite.com

TweetDeck
www.tweetdeck.com

The Unofficial Index to Educational Twitter Hashtags
https://docs.google.com/a/giftedhomeschoolers.org/document/d
/1CkUrFNr3ZThZXLh4kwk9rk-wQlwfcg8YL9zVx1R_C2s/edit#

Twitter Accounts to Check Out

Please note that Twitter accounts, like much on the Internet, change frequently. These handles were active at time of publication. Gifted Homeschoolers Forum and Engaging Educators are not responsible for the content of individual accounts.

Twitter Accounts to Get Started

@engaginged   @GiftedHF

Gifted- and 2e-related Twitter Accounts

@GiftedHF   @ljconrad
@laughingatchaos   @gtchatmod
@DavidsonGifted   @IEAgifted
@prufrockpress   @GiftedDevCenter
@LesLinks   @SENG_Gifted
@HoagiesGifted   @ThinkKids
@drseide

Homeschool-related Twitter Accounts

@secularhs   @TammyT
@DianeFlynnKeith   @JimmiesCollage
@homeschoolblogs   @HipHmschoolMoms
@noagendaHS   @iHomeschoolNet
@prachomeschool   @campcreek

@ABCMoms   @parentatthehelm
@homeschoolDB   @TheHomeschool
@dazeofadventure   @homeschoolDTW
@homeschoolcrew   @hmhomeschoolers
@thehsvillage   @upsidedownHS

@startsateight   @HomeCurriculum
@HSClassroom   @thekidshouldsee
@wonderopolis

Education-related Twitter Accounts

@engaginged   @rmbyrne
@thinkwell   @NASAJPL_Edu
@googlescifair   @SciAfterSchool
@SesameWorkshop   @GrammarGirl
@MathDude

URL Shorteners

http://bit.ly

http://goo.gl

http://tinyurl.com

Engaging Educators Video Tutorials

http://www.engagingeducators.com/tutorial-videos.html

About the Authors

Ben Curran

Ben was born and raised in Pontiac, Michigan. He earned his teaching degree from Eastern Michigan University and began his teaching career in 2000. Since then, he has taught, at various times, grades four through eight. He is currently employed as an instructional coach at a charter school in Detroit, Michigan. In addition, he teaches (along with his co-author) educational technology workshops for his district.

In 2011, Ben and Neil founded Engaging Educators, a company dedicated to helping educators and families transform their learning environments in meaningful and exciting ways. Ben blogs actively for Engaging Educators at engagingeducators.com/blog, as well as for his school at upaet.blogspot.com and about poetry at thesmallnouns.blogspot.com.

Ben lives outside Detroit with his wife, daughter, and two sons.

Neil Wetherbee

Neil grew up in Northport, Michigan, a small town outside of Traverse City. The public school district he attended was a member of the Coalition of Essential Schools. His relationship with the educational process was significantly shaped by the high expectations, personalization, and performance-based assessments found in these schools. He earned his teaching degree from the University of Michigan and has been teaching in a Detroit charter school since 2005.

More and more of Neil's teaching included the use of technology, so he sought formal training in the field of educational technology. He earned an Educational Technology Certificate and an M.A. in educational technology from Michigan State University. He regularly implements Web 2.0 technologies with an emphasis on course management systems to increase student engagement and achievement. To continue his growth in the field of educational technology, Neil is a member of the International Society for Technology in Education. Look for his upcoming book from Eye on Education (www.eyeoneducation.com), which he also co-authored with Ben.

Neil currently lives in Rochester, Michigan, with his wife and three young daughters.